EASY PIANO

W9-C?A-202

Simply Broadway

18 Favorite Selections
from Classic Broadway Musicals

Arranged by Dan Coates

Simply Broadway is a collection of classic hits from the greatest Broadway musicals. These songs have been carefully selected and arranged by Dan Coates for Easy Piano, making them accessible to pianists of all ages. Phrase markings, articulations, fingering, pedaling and dynamics have been included to aid with interpretation, and a large print size makes the notation easy to read.

Music is at the heart of every Broadway show. Through each musical number, the audience learns about what drives the characters on stage. The songs they sing reveal their deepest thoughts—their loves and hates, their dreams and memories. As a result of this and the talent of some of the world's greatest composers and lyricists, Broadway has been the source for many great songs. Many of these have become standards and have been recorded by famous artists. Also, many Broadway shows have been adapted for the big screen and have become popular musical films. Whether jazzy, sassy, lyrical, nostalgic, whimsical, vivacious, peppy, romantic, or joyful, these songs are a pleasure to play on the piano. With its ability to make us laugh, cry and sometimes tap our feet, Broadway music has been embraced by musicians and audiences, young and old, around the world. For these reasons and more, the following pages are exciting to explore.

After all, this is *Simply Broadway!*

ISBN-10: 0-7390-5354-X
ISBN-13: 978-0-7390-5354-6

Contents

Anything Goes

from *Anything Goes*

Words and Music by Cole Porter
Arranged by Dan Coates

4

And All That Jazz

from *Chicago*

Lyrics by Fred Ebb
Music by John Kander
Arranged by Dan Coates

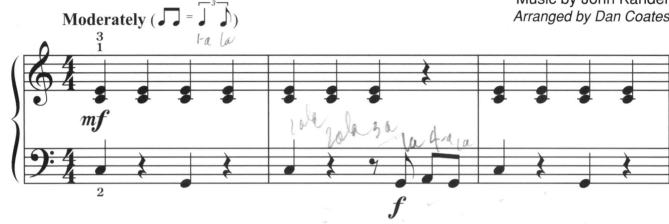

Start the car,— I know a / Hold on, hon,— we're gon-na

whoop-ee spot— where the / bun-ny hug,— I bought some

gin is cold— but the pi- / as-pi-rin— down at U-

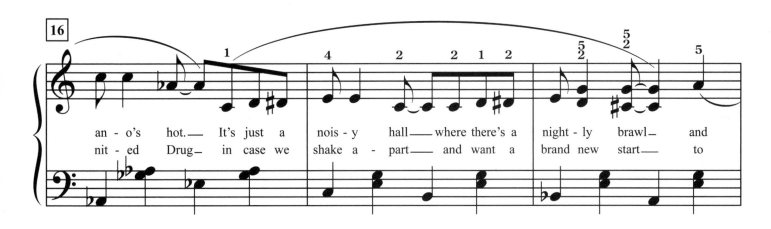

an - o's hot.— It's just a / nit - ed Drug— in case we

nois - y hall— where there's a / shake a - part— and want a

night - ly brawl— and / brand new start— to

all / do

that / that

1.

jazz!

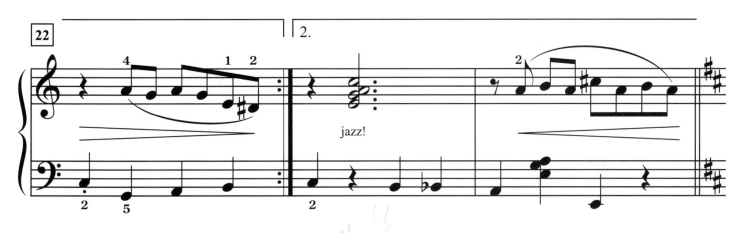

2.

jazz!

25

f Oh, I'm gon - na see my She - ba shim - my shake.— (And

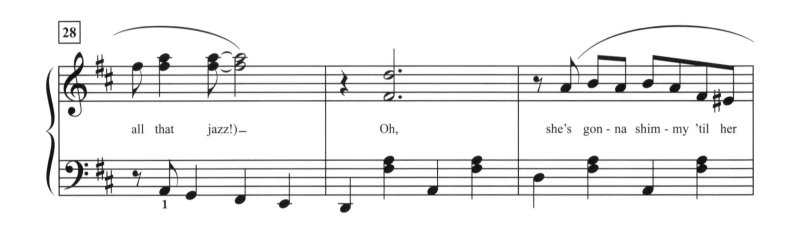

28

all that jazz!)— Oh, she's gon - na shim - my 'til her

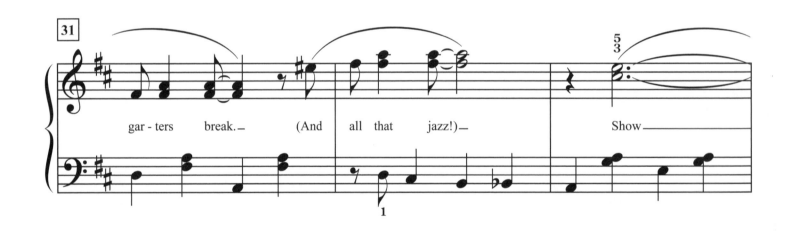

31

gar - ters break.— (And all that jazz!)— Show

34

—— her where to park her gir - dle, oh,——— her moth - er's blood - 'd cur - dle

if she'd hear— her ba - by's queer— for all
dim.
mp

that *f* jazz!

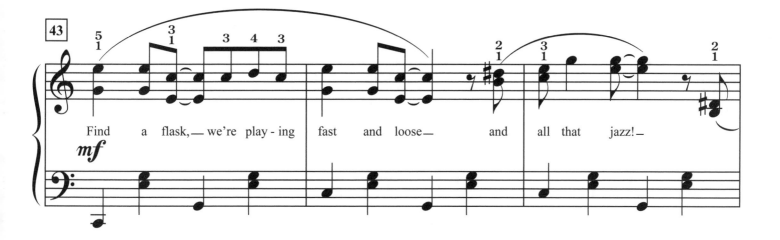

mf
Find a flask,— we're play - ing fast and loose— and all that jazz!—

Right up here— is where I store the juice,— and

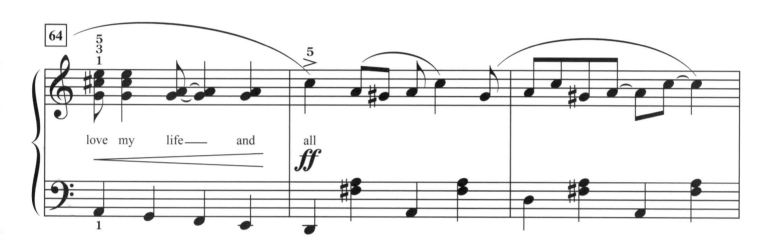

Don't Rain on My Parade

from *Funny Girl*

Words by Bob Merrill
Music by Jule Styne
Arranged by Dan Coates

march, my heart's— a drum-mer. Don't bring— a-round a cloud to rain— on my pa-

rade._____ *dim.* I'm gon - na live and— live now!

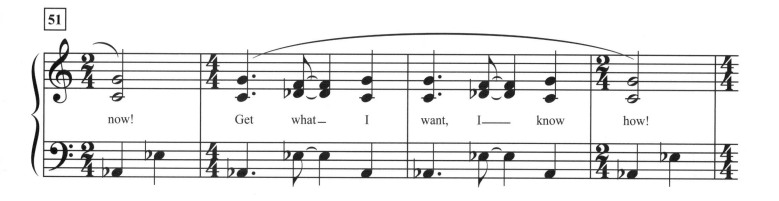

now! Get what— I want, I— know how!

All that— the law will— al - low! *cresc.* One roll— for *mf*

16

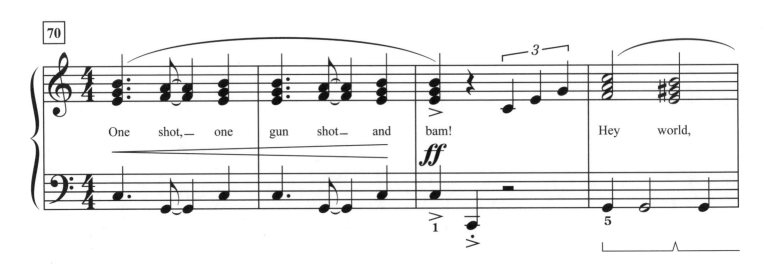

Diamonds Are a Girl's Best Friend

from *Gentlemen Prefer Blondes*

Words by Leo Robin
Music by Jule Styne
Arranged by Dan Coates

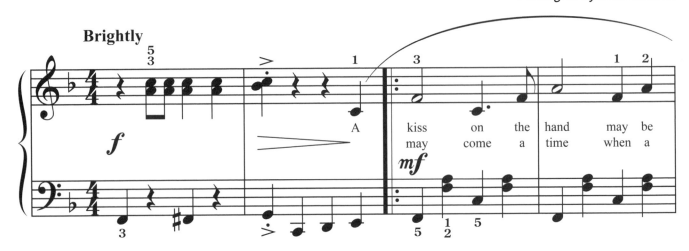

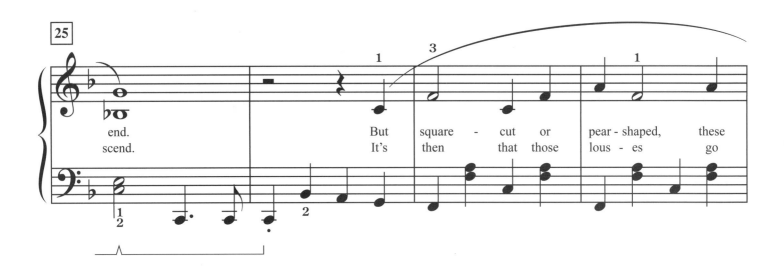

end.
scend.
But square - cut or pear - shaped, these
It's then that those lous - es go

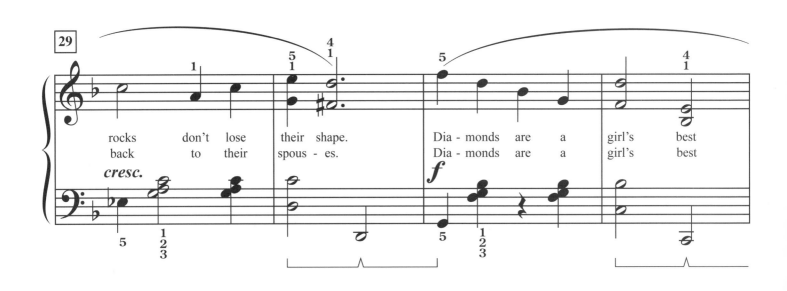

rocks don't lose their shape.
back to lose their spous - es.
Dia - monds are a girl's best
Dia - monds are a girl's best

cresc.

f

1.
2.

friend.
There
friend.

sfz

Ease On Down the Road

from *The Wiz*

Words and Music by
Charlie Smalls
Arranged by Dan Coates

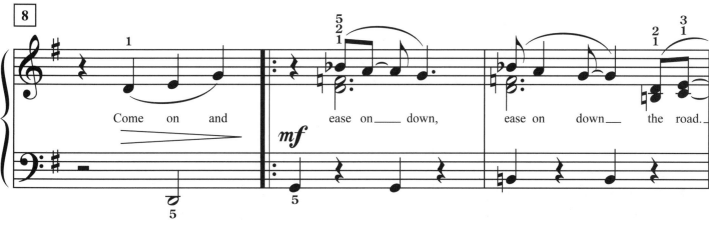

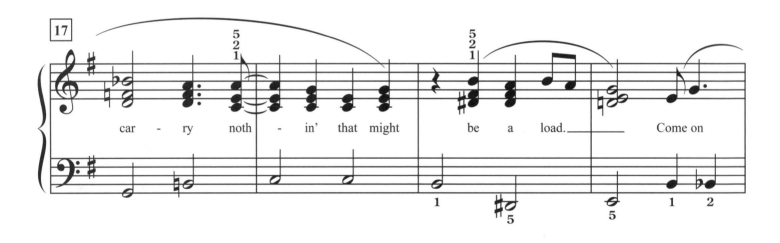

24

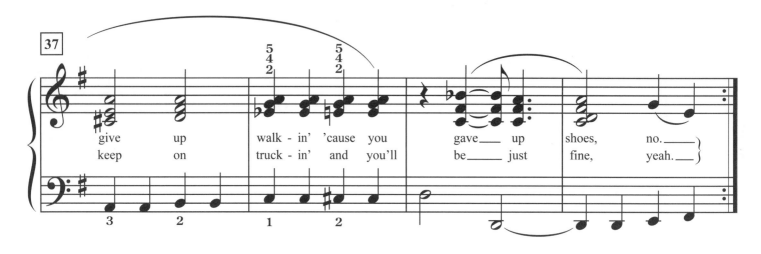

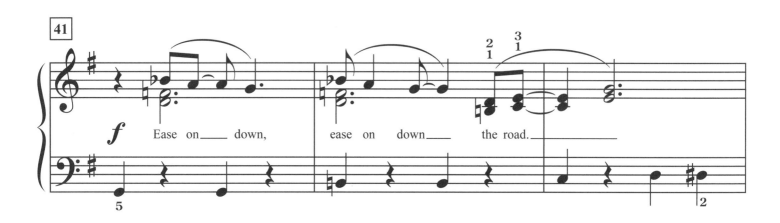

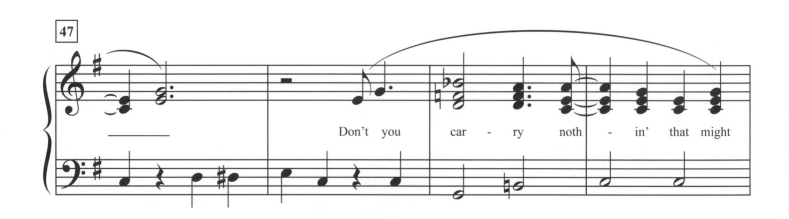

Heart

from *Damn Yankees*

Words and Music by
Richard Adler and Jerry Ross
Arranged by Dan Coates

So In Love

from *Kiss Me, Kate*

Words and Music by
Cole Porter
Arranged by Dan Coates

Slowly, with passion

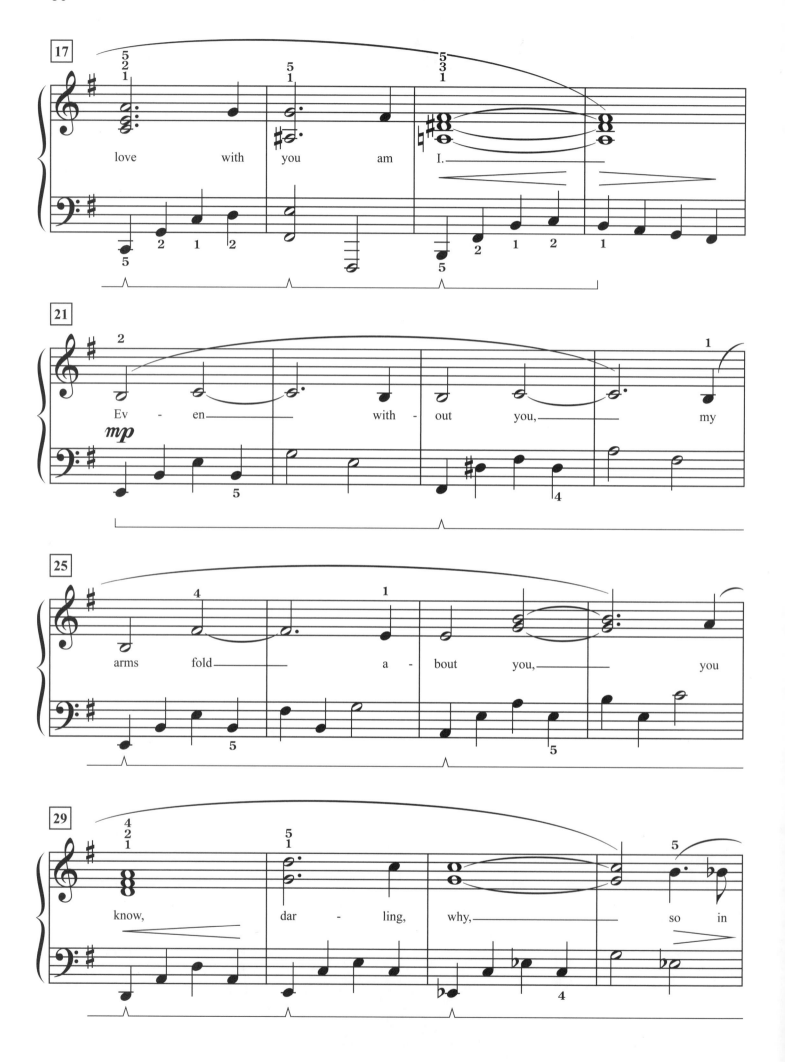

love, _____ so in love, _____ so in love with you, my love, _____ am

mf dim. poco a poco

mp

rit. e dim.

p

pp

Hey There

from *The Pajama Game*

Words and Music by
Richard Adler and Jerry Ross
Arranged by Dan Coates

Moderately slow, with expression

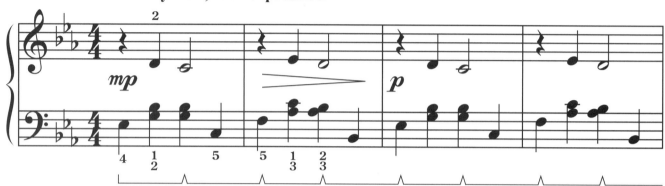

Hey there,———— you with the stars in your eyes,

love nev-er made a fool of you, you used to be too

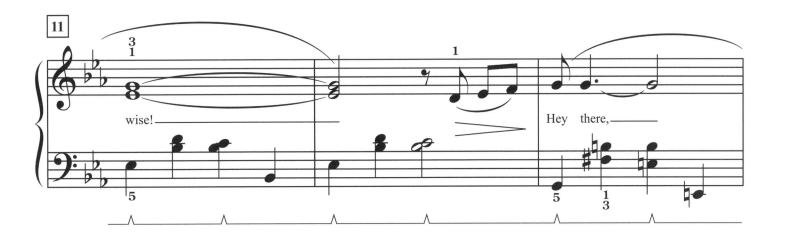

wise! _____ Hey there, _____

you on that high fly - ing cloud, though she won't throw a

crumb to you, you think some - day she'll come to you.

Bet - ter for - get her, _____ her with her nose in the air.

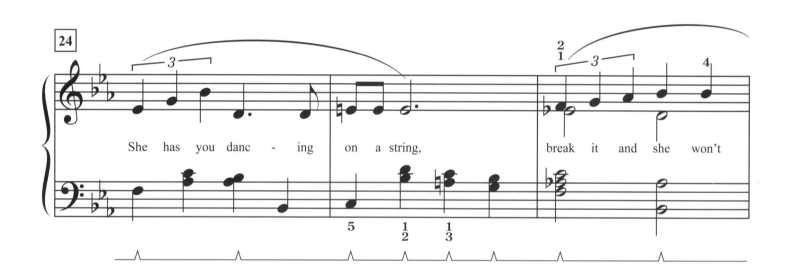

She has you danc - ing on a string, break it and she won't

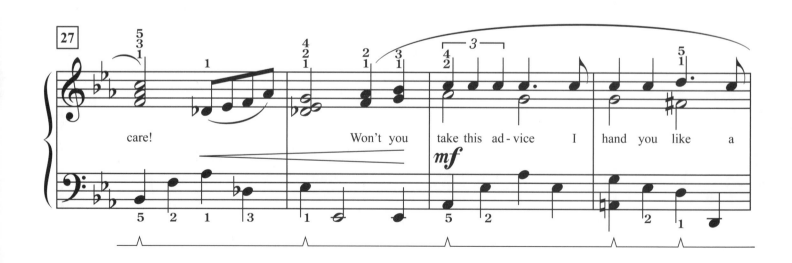

care! Won't you take this ad - vice I hand you like a

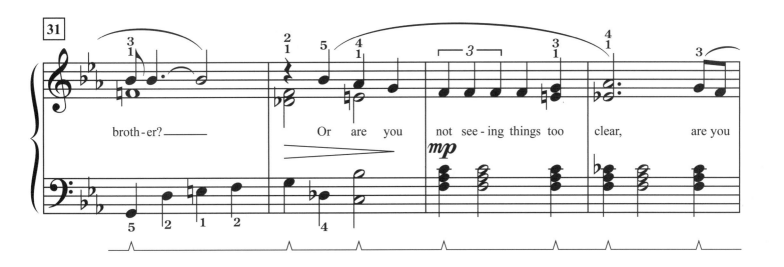

broth-er?_____ Or are you not see-ing things too clear, are you

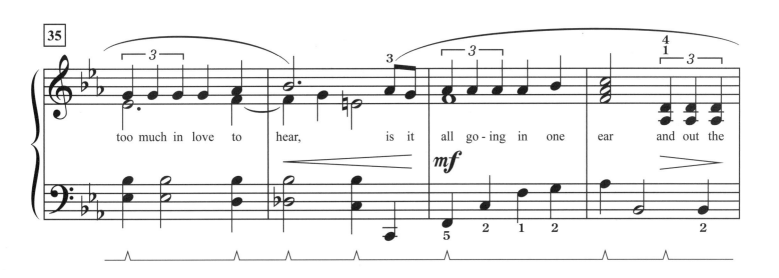

too much in love to hear, is it all go-ing in one ear and out the

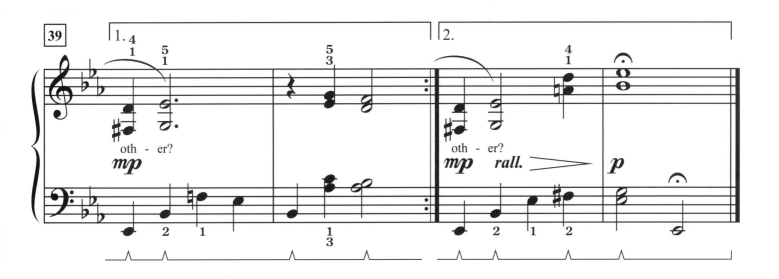

oth - er? oth - er?

How Are Things in Glocca Morra?

from *Finian's Rainbow*

Words by E.Y. Harburg
Music by Burton Lane
Arranged by Dan Coates

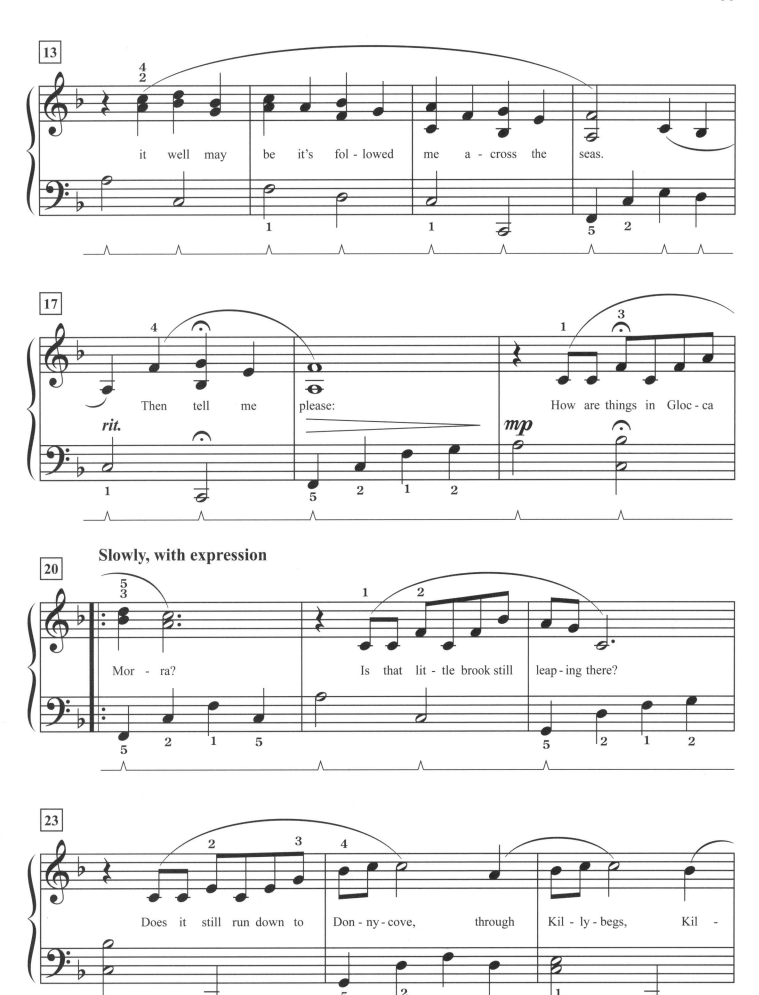

How Could I Ever Know?

from *The Secret Garden*

Lyrics by Marsha Norman
Music by Lucy Simon
Arranged by Dan Coates

I Could Have Danced All Night

from *My Fair Lady*

Lyrics by Alan Jay Lerner
Music by Frederick Loewe
Arranged by Dan Coates

48

If Ever I Would Leave You

from *Camelot*

Music by Frederick Loewe
Lyrics by Alan Jay Lerner
Arranged by Dan Coates

Slowly, with expression

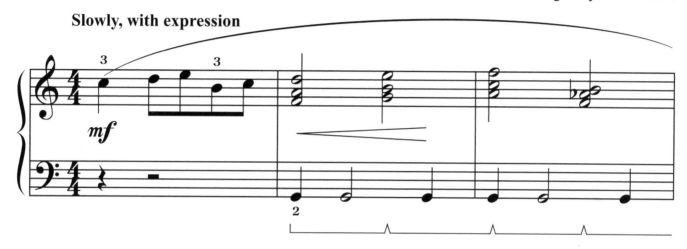

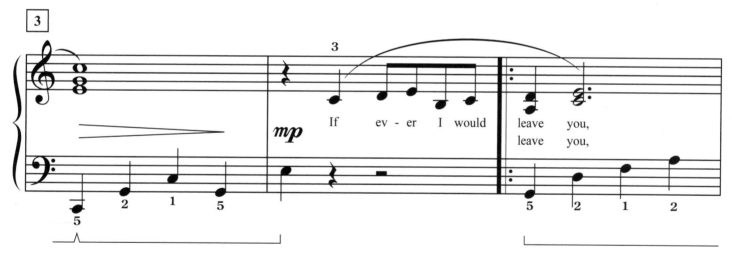

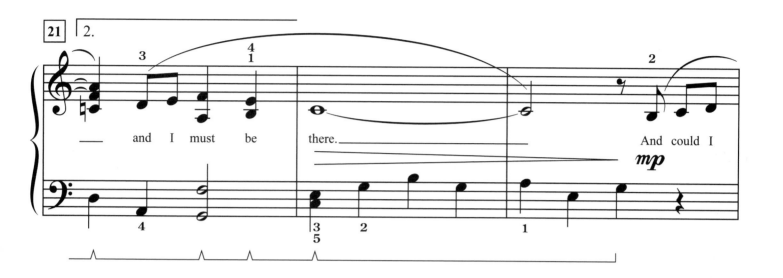

and I must be there._____ And could I

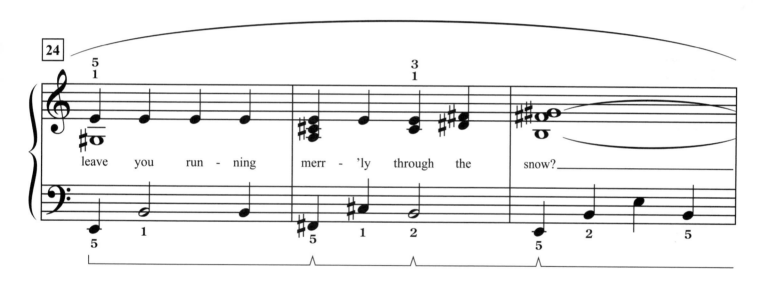

leave you run - ning merr - 'ly through the snow?_____

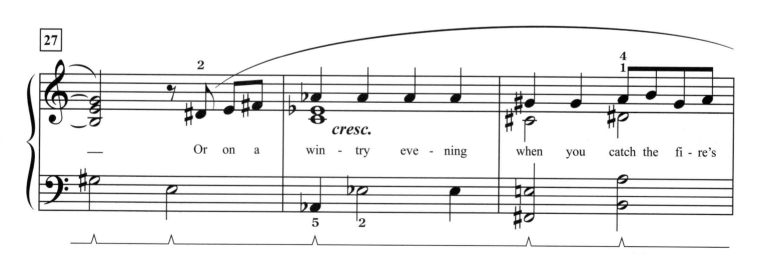

Or on a win - try eve - ning when you catch the fi - re's

54

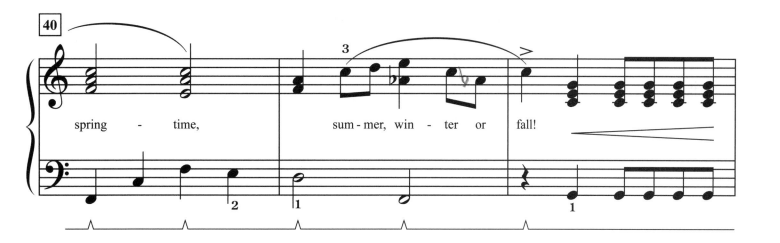

spring - time,   sum - mer, win - ter or   fall!

No,   nev - er could I   leave   you_____   at

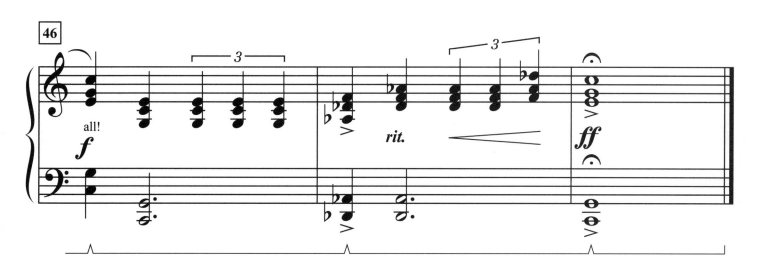

all!

I Won't Grow Up

from *Peter Pan*

Lyrics by Carolyn Leigh
Music by Mark Charlap
Arranged by Dan Coates

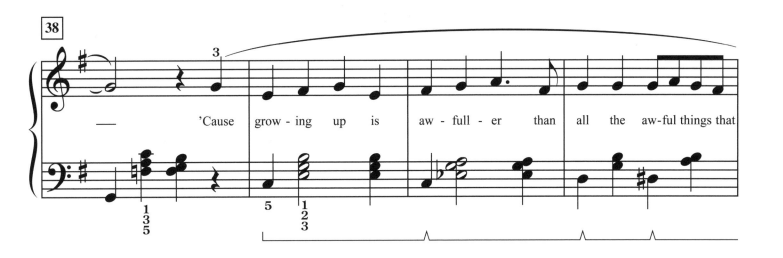

'Cause grow-ing up is aw-full-er than all the aw-ful things that

ev - er were. I'll nev-er grow up, nev-er grow up, nev-er grow up,—— no

sir, not I, not me, I won't, no sir!

Mack the Knife

from *The Threepenny Opera*

Music by Kurt Weill
English Words by Marc Blitzstein
Original German Words by Bert Brecht
Arranged by Dan Coates

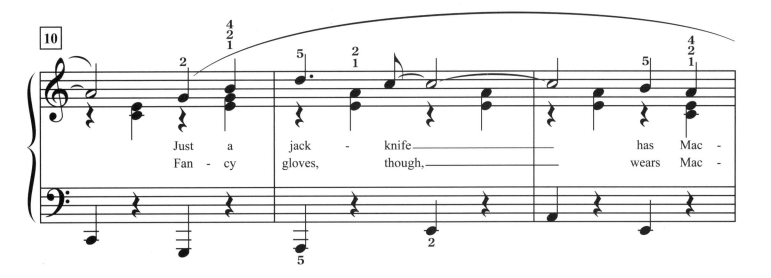

62

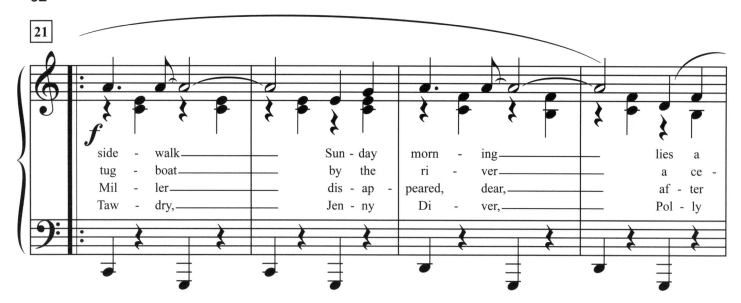

side - walk_____ Sun - day morn - ing_____ lies a
tug - boat_____ by the ri - ver_____ a ce -
Mil - ler_____ dis - ap - peared, dear,_____ af - ter
Taw - dry,_____ Jen - ny Di - ver,_____ Pol - ly

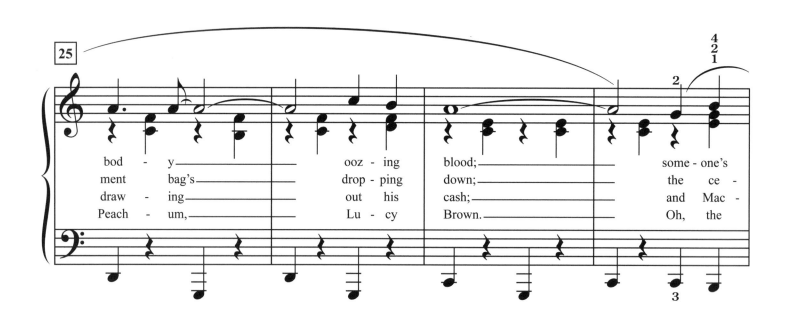

bod - y_____ ooz - ing blood;_____ some - one's
ment bag's_____ drop - ping down;_____ the ce -
draw - ing_____ out his cash;_____ and Mac -
Peach - um,_____ Lu - cy Brown._____ Oh, the

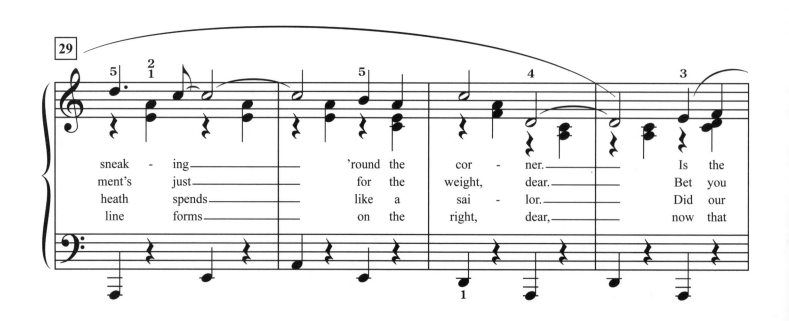

sneak - ing_____ 'round the cor - ner._____ Is the
ment's just_____ for the weight, dear._____ Bet you
heath spends_____ like a sai - lor._____ Did our
line forms_____ on the right, dear,_____ now that

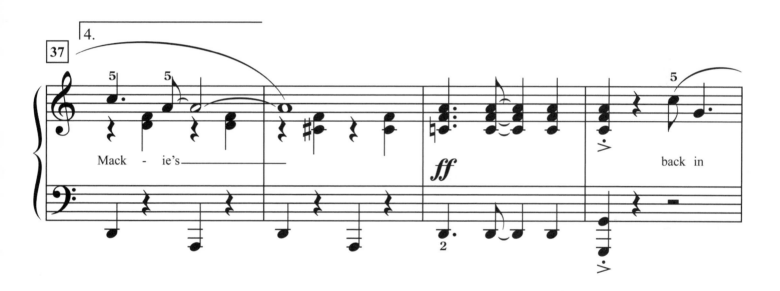

Not While I'm Around

from *Sweeney Todd*

Music and Lyrics by
Stephen Sondheim
Arranged by Dan Coates

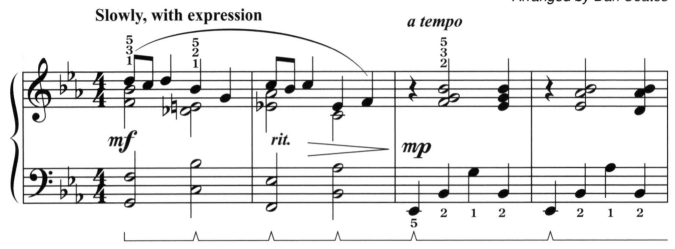

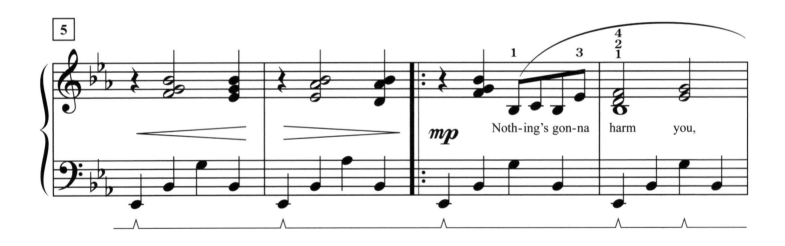

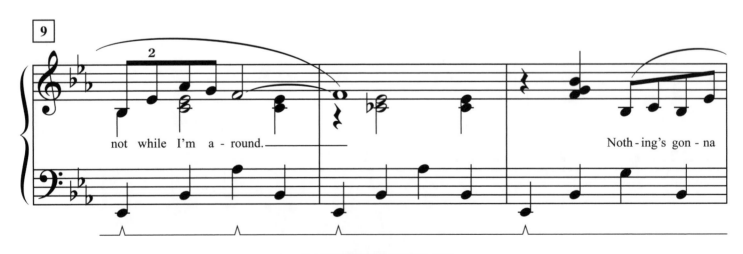

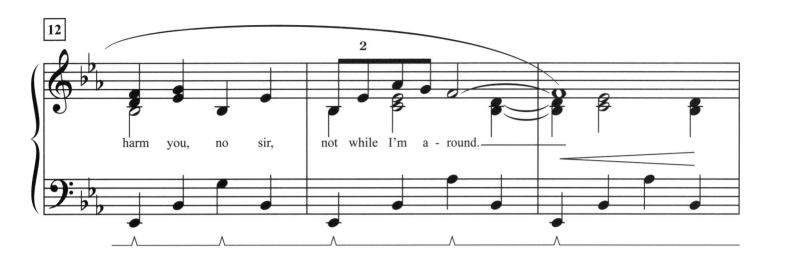

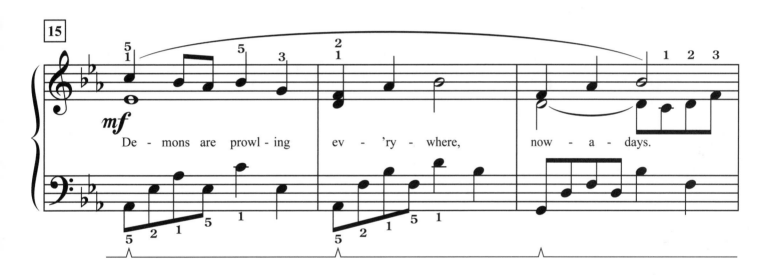

De - mons'll charm you with a smile for a - while, but in time,

f

rit.

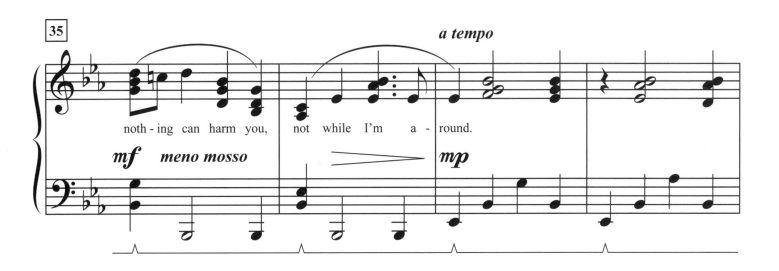

a tempo

noth - ing can harm you, not while I'm a - round.

mf *meno mosso* *mp*

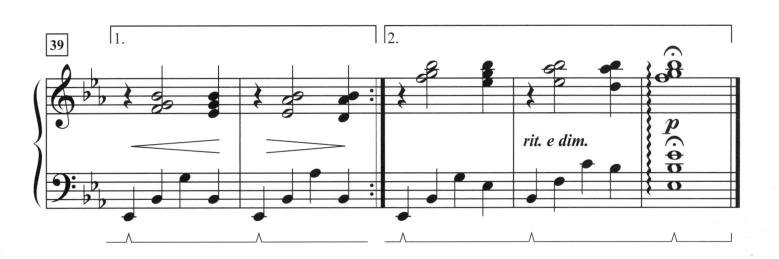

1.

2.

rit. e dim.

p

Summertime

from *Porgy and Bess*

Music and Lyrics by George Gershwin,
Du Bose and Dorothy Heyward and Ira Gershwin
Arranged by Dan Coates

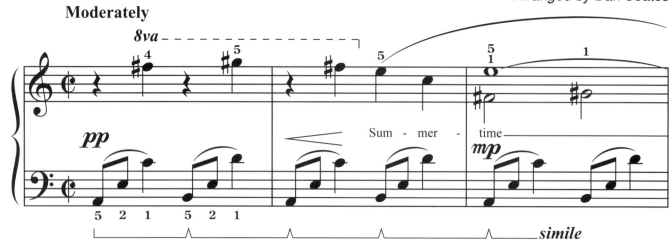

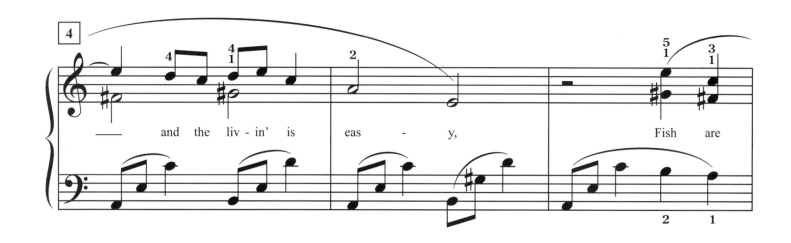

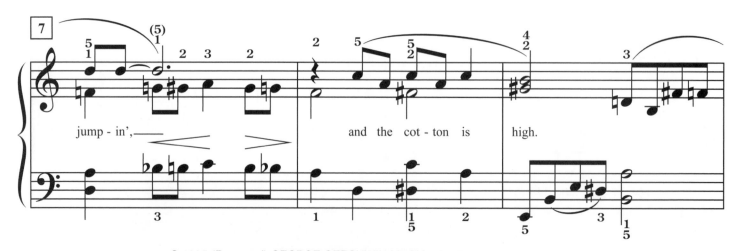

Oh, your dad-dy's rich,— and your ma is good-

look - in', So hush, lit - tle ba - by,

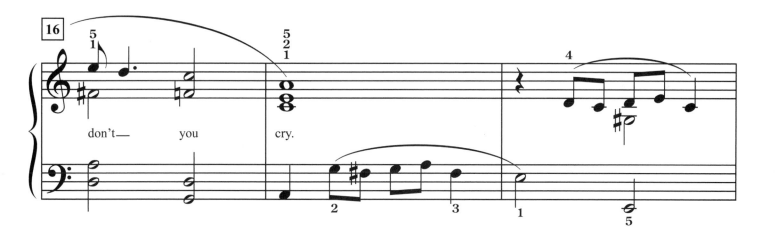

don't— you cry.

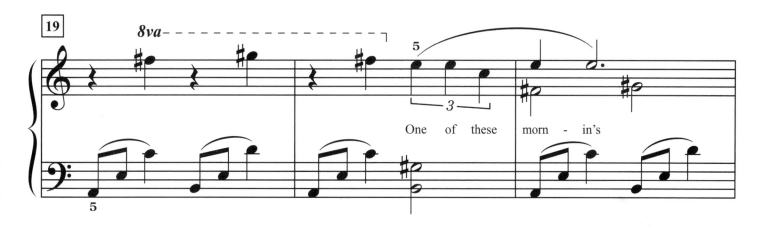

8va

One of these morn - in's

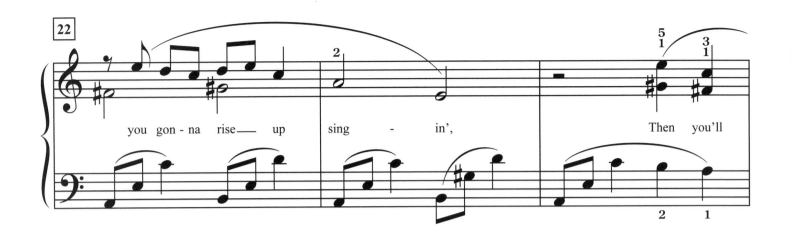

22
you gon - na rise —— up sing - in', Then you'll

25
spread your wings and you'll take to the sky.

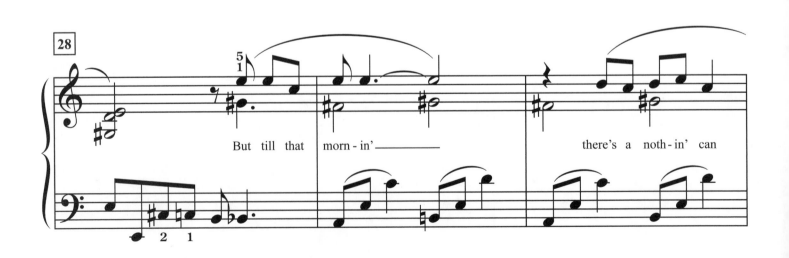

28
But till that morn - in' ———— there's a noth - in' can

harm you

With Dad - dy and Mam - my

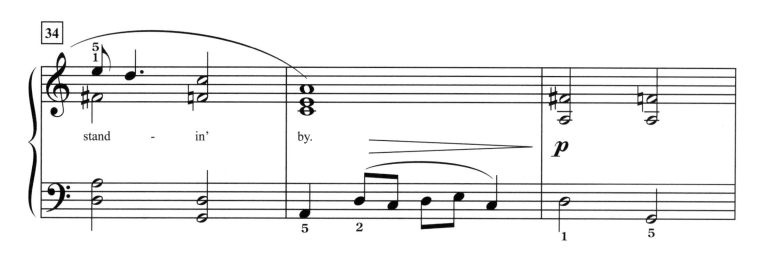

stand - in' by.

p

pp *rit.*

Together Wherever We Go

from *Gypsy*

Lyrics by Stephen Sondheim
Music by Jule Styne
Arranged by Dan Coates

Brightly, in two

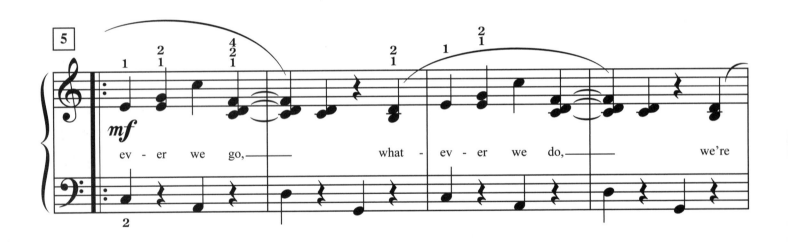

74

Ragtime

from *Ragtime*

Lyrics by Lynn Ahrens
Music by Stephen Flaherty
Arranged by Dan Coates

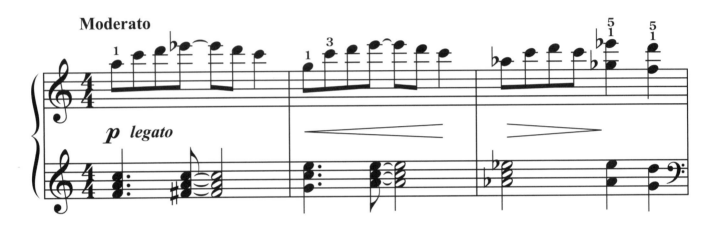

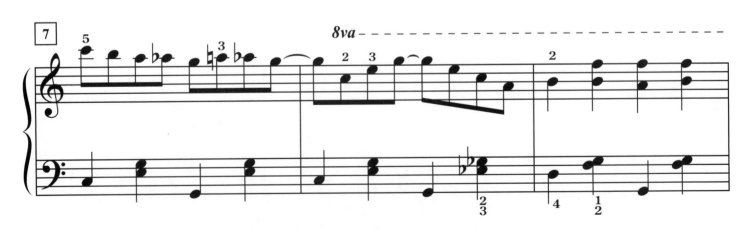

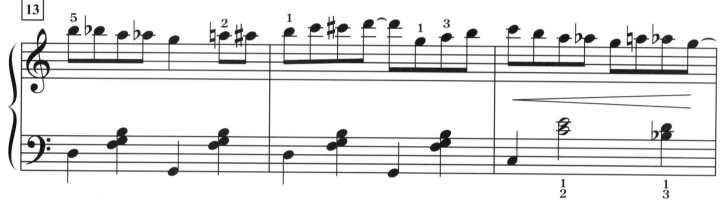

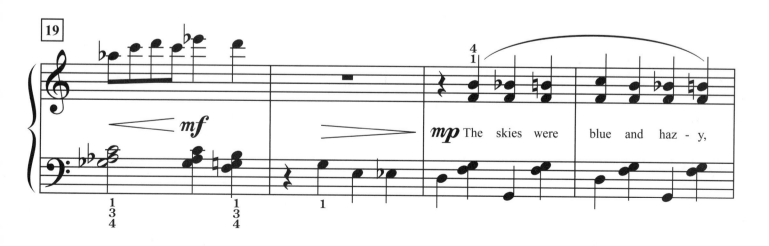

mp The skies were blue and haz - y,

rare-ly a storm,— bare-ly a chill. La - la-la-la - la! The af - ter - noons were la - zy,

ev'-ry-one warm,— ev'ry- thing still. La - la-la-la - la! And there was dis - tant mu - sic,

cresc.

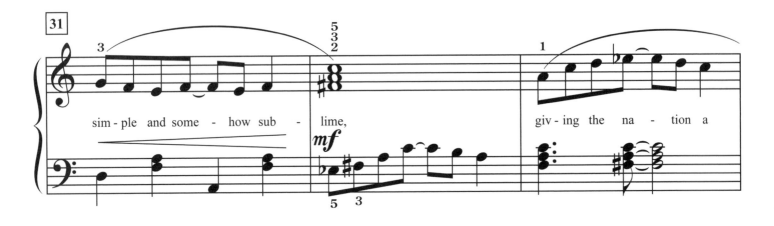

sim - ple and some - how sub - lime, *mf* giv-ing the na - tion a

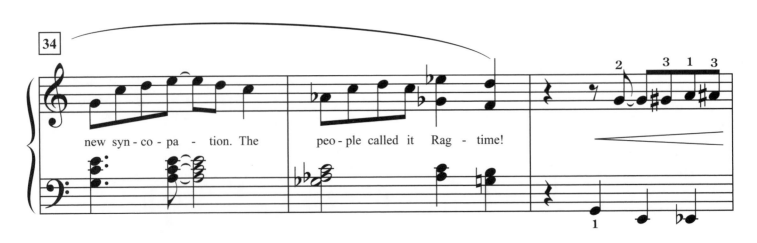

new syn-co-pa - tion. The peo-ple called it Rag - time!